P/99

Burningham - John Burningham

95391
cl 88

Copyright © 1985 by John Burningham
All rights reserved. No part of this book may be reproduced
or transmitted in any form or by any means, electronic or mechanical,
including photocopying, recording, or by any information storage
and retrieval system, without permission in writing from the publisher.
Originally published in Great Britain by
Walker Books, Ltd., 184–192 Drummond Street, London NW1 3HP
Published in the United States in 1986 by Crown Publishers, Inc.,
225 Park Avenue South, New York, New York 10003
CROWN is a trademark of Crown Publishers, Inc.
IT'S GREAT TO LEARN!   and logo
are trademarks of Crown Publishers, Inc.
Manufactured in Italy

Library of Congress Cataloging in Publication Data
Burningham, John.   John Burningham's Opposites.
Summary: Introduces the concept of opposites
through labeled pictures of a boy interacting with a
thin pig and fat pig, a hot dragon and a cold snowman,
and other creatures and situations.
1. Vocabulary—Juvenile literature.   2. English
language—Synonyms and antonyms—Juvenile literature.
[1. Vocabulary.   2. English language—Synonyms and
antonyms]   I. Title.   II. Title; Opposites.
PE1449.B864   1986   428.1   85-13218
ISBN 0-517-55963-3
10 9 8 7 6 5 4 3 2 1
First American Edition

# John Burningham's
# Opposites

CROWN PUBLISHERS, INC.     NEW YORK

# dry

# wet

# hard

# soft

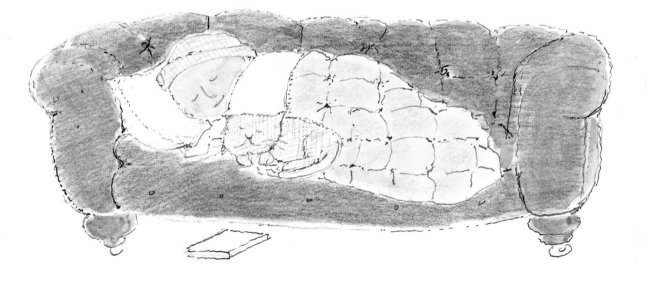

heavy

light

# noisy

# quiet

# hot

cold

slow

fast

young

old

big

# little

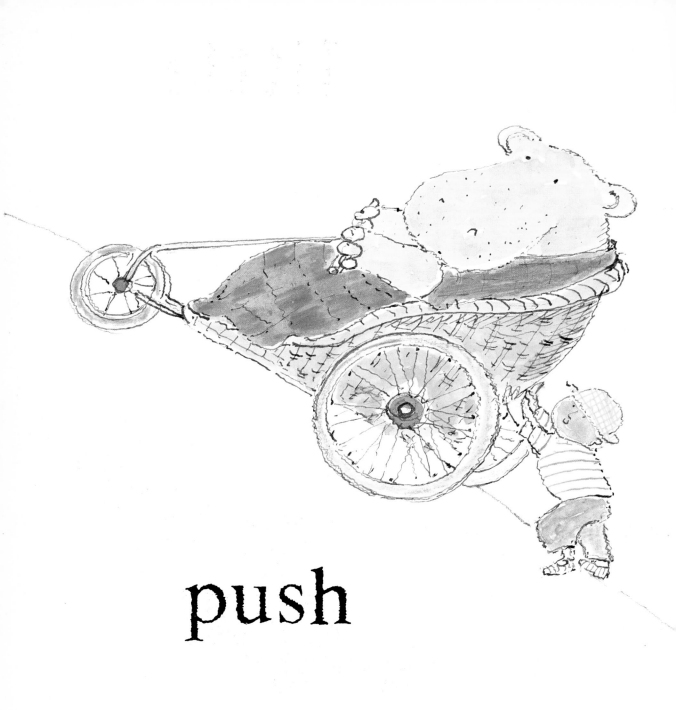

push

pull

up

down

# thin

# fat

# open

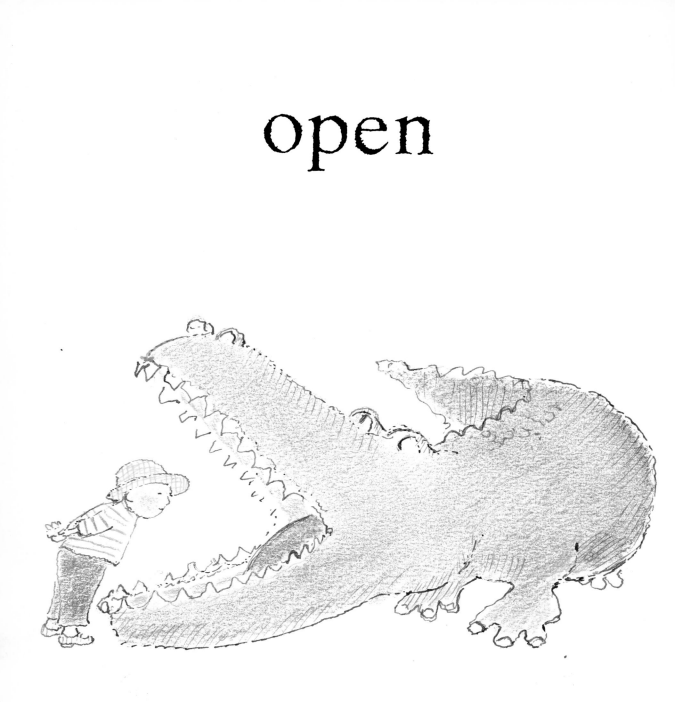

# shut